Ozana Giusca

Business Unlimited
Smarter Profits Faster

- Volume 3 -

Increase Internal Efficiency

101 Zero-Cost Tactics to Take Your Company to the Next Level

Amaze Yourself With What YOU Can Achieve Further!

Copyright © 2017 Ozana Giusca
All rights reserved.

ISBN-13: 978-1978361850
ISBN-10: 1978361858

To all the business owners and entrepreneurs I have worked with: thank you for entrusting me with growing your business.

To my team, who have put so much effort into building Tooliers, the high-end business growth tools and programs that are transforming businesses around the world, a big thank you for going through the ups and downs with me.

Thank you for helping me with this book. We wouldn't be here without your dedication and contribution!

I would like to name the Tooliers core team: Vali, Dragos, Sorana & Catalina. You are like family to me! I am so grateful you joined me in my journey!

Table of Contents

Foreword	V
Preface	VII
My Story	IX
Introduction	1
Bonus • Steady Growth - Systematize Your Business	4
Tactic #1 • Follow a System	5
Note: Tactics #2- #31 are in Volumes 1-2	
Increase Internal Efficiency	12
Tactic #32 • Automate Processes	13
Tactic #33 • Plan the Day	16
Tactic #34 • Use Meetings	20
Tactic #35 • Use an Agenda at Meetings	23
Tactic #36 • Be Efficient with Your Time	28
Tactic #37 • Strengthen the Weakest Link	32
Tactic #38 • Eliminate Wasting Time in Routine Tasks	36
Tactic #39 • Get Used to Delegating	40
Tactic #40 • Give People the Right Tools When Delegating	44
Tactic #41 • Get a Reporting System in Place	48
Tactic #42 • Measure Everything and Continuously Improve	51
Tactic #43 • Have an Organizational Chart	56
Tactic #44 • Have a Consistency System in Place	59
Smart Business System™	64
Bonus • Love Letter	76
Love Letter Template	78
Love Letter Example	79
Glossary of Terms	82

Foreword

The world is changing so fast. These events are opportunities for those who grab them, and at the same time can negatively affect those who do not take action. Most small businesses find it harder to break through their current level. They reach a plateau and do not know what step to take next, or go beyond 'small' and lose the plot.

There is so much information available now about how to run a successful business, but the challenge is to find meaning within this information and to use it appropriately to optimize and grow your business. In my experience as a small business consultant, I have seen a lot of business owners who cannot simply and quickly explain what they do, let alone generate interest and sell their products or services. I also see that entrepreneurs have dreams and goals, yet 80% of their time is spent on things that have no link whatsoever with their objectives. If they do not focus on what is needed to achieve their goals, how can they get there?

If you are looking for a very hands-on approach to building your business from the ground up, Ozana has nailed it in *Business Unlimited*. What a purposeful read for anyone who is an entrepreneur or small business owner. As you continue on your business or career journey, you will face real challenges that may deter you from achieving your biggest goals. The tactics in this book will keep you on track and help you reach your goals in record time.

In our lives we have the opportunity to do it the hard way or to learn from what the experts do, and then do it better. Ozana has been trained by some of the best in the business, including business and marketing guru Jay Abraham. In this new book you will discover key observations and ingredients to create even more success in your life and business. The real-world examples, as well as the practical exercises at the end of each tactic, also ensure this is a user-friendly manual to reaching business success.

Foreword

In *Business Unlimited*, you will learn to see the bigger picture of your business as well as discover the importance of *systematically* improving it; that is, by prioritizing and focusing on those areas that most need improvement. You will learn to identify your best customers; let go of any customers who do not lift your business; learn from your competitors; and fulfil the core purpose of every business: providing *real value* to your customers. You will also discover how creating the right kind of partnerships will grow your business with little extra effort on your part. Business owners will find the tactics on closing sales and creating urgency especially valuable. You will also see how essential it is to build relationships both with your best customers and your team.

This book is also brutally honest about areas in which business owners tend to waste time and resources – and provides a wealth of best practices for time management; this includes a reminder to employ the time-saving advantages of certain technologies. You will also be encouraged to reflect and act upon your role as a leader and to go beyond merely managing your business to making sure it leads to the kind of life and lifestyle you desire. Aspects like personal branding, networking and being open to change are also discussed. Finally, you will clarify your vision in order to take your brand into the future and be left with a business that is dynamic and that constantly strives for – and achieves – improvement and growth.

The bottom line: if you are ready to increase your success rate today, take the time to read this mind-expanding book two to three times, and then implement the ideas that are shared here.

Bill Walsh

America's Small Business Expert

Website: billwalsh360.com

Preface

If you answer YES! to any of these statements, this book is for you.

- You have achieved some success with your business, but seem unable to grow it further.
- You are not satisfied with where your business is.
- You are not getting enough from your business (you are not getting enough recognition or enough money, or you have not succeeded in fully achieving your Objectives).
- Work is taking over your life and you have no time for family, relaxation, or travel.
- You are still struggling to make a living.
- You are bored with your work! You want something more challenging and fun.
- You are missing something, but you're not sure exactly what.
- There are some areas you do not understand (for example, finance) or you are passionate about your product, but you cannot sell it.
- You just want to be sure that you are on top of things and that your business is on the right track.
- You have some ideas for new businesses, but are not quite sure how to go about it.
- You want new challenges, but you need your current business to continue to run for various reasons (financial, community).
- Your turnover and/or profits have started decreasing.
- You can anticipate a disaster but you cannot tell what exactly is happening.
- Your best employees have started to leave.
- You have lost your biggest client.
- You seem to deliver good quality but your clients are still not prepared to pay what you'd like for your products.
- There has been a recent change in your company's industry or outside

Preface

environment and this has had a great impact on your business.
- You and your staff are working too hard and it is just not fair on any of you (especially given the results you achieve).
- You consider your company a victim of your crisis, a system, or something else.
- Your business has stopped serving the community.
- Your business is growing quickly and you are struggling to manage it. It is becoming too complex for you to run on your own.
- Your life is too stressful. There are just too many problems that need to be solved by you, the business owner.
- You and your co-owners have trouble running the business together.
- Your business has started experiencing problems or you foresee problems, but you don't know what to do about them.
- You have accumulated too much debt in your company and can no longer sustain it.
- You simply want to discover the latest strategies that Fortune 500 companies use for their success!

My Story

I want to take a few minutes to ask you the questions that are on every small business owner's mind:

- What is the REAL secret behind businesses that generate more profits while their owners are enjoying life and doing what they want, when they want?
- Can I get more customers to call us instead of *us* chasing *them*?
- How can I get a great team of committed employees to work hard so we grow the business together?
- Is there any way to feel happier with my business and really achieve what I set my mind to?
- Ultimately, how can I, a small business owner, entrepreneur or freelance expert, make a difference in the world?

I get asked these questions all the time and it's why I wrote this book. Via this book, the tools, programs, events we deliver, I provide the answers to these questions, and many more.

Before you dig in, let me tell you a little about myself…

In 2007 my life seemed perfect. I was a rising star, doing everything most people would love to do.

After attaining my MBA from Cass Business School, London in 2000, I worked in the City for a few years. In 2003, I set up my own consulting firm, where I advised on selling a few companies and raised hundreds of millions in bank finance for various projects.

While my business generated a decent income, I knew I was on my way to support other entrepreneurs help more people and make a bigger impact.

With a team of 12 consultants, I was living my dream. I could party, travel, wear my favorite brands…

My Story

I bought a flat, then another one, then an office for our company, a new car... until the financial crisis hit my business badly, as happened with thousands of businesses around the world.

All of a sudden money stopped flowing in. The banks withdrew from financing our transactions; those hundreds of thousands of dollars in success fees never arrived; and ongoing consulting projects got put on hold. No more new business meant no more cash.

Imagine: By January 2009, I had let most of my team go. For me, they were not just staff, they were *family*. And they were damn good at what they did.

With more than a million dollars in debt, I could no longer pay the bank. Many sleepless nights followed... I felt ashamed, convinced people would point a finger at me, accuse me of not paying my debts. I got scared thinking about a potential bad credit rating and that I might never be able to get a loan again.

I felt my reputation as an honest, trustworthy businessperson was ruined as I couldn't pay my debts.

I had no money coming in and was borrowing on a monthly basis to pay my two remaining staff members. I was driving to my father every weekend to get food for the week for me and my partner.

It seemed that every phone call I got, every email I received, brought more bad news.

Watch this: my phone service provider threatening to end my contract should I not pay my bills. Imagine trying to save a business without a phone connection or access to the internet!

That was it, I decided. *Enough!* I borrowed more money and paid for an event in London where 15 successful entrepreneurs shared their strategies on how they became profitable. I learned about online marketing, selling one-to-many via events and social media advertising. Most importantly I realized the need to be visible to the right audience.

How many of these tactics do you think I applied? None! Because I soon realized I was in the wrong business anyway. Yep, this was my biggest take-away from the conference. I realized there was nothing special about me or my business, nothing that would get clients to choose our services.

There were too many people doing the same thing, making it difficult to differentiate myself.

As I had all this cutting edge knowledge, I started applying it to the businesses of former clients, and friends. And *this* is how I started earning again…

It turned out my consulting business was not the only business lacking proper business knowledge! In fact, most small businesses lack such knowledge – they are usually set up based on an opportunity the founder sees, based on the founder's skills and abilities. Yet businesses are complex and no entrepreneur can know it all; certainly no one can handle everything.

I also discovered my special gift: being able to identify where a business is leaving money on the table and how they can double or even triple their profits by making a few important changes.

My skill became immediately obvious as I managed to achieve:

- **30% increase in Sales within a month** for a client in hospitality (hotel) and a **287% increase in their online bookings within three months.** Their occupancy rate was 10% when we started working together – now it's in excess of 50%.

- **8 Sales during the first workshop** for a weight loss solution – a full house event achieved within five days of promotion. In fact, we had to close the doors and leave people outside disappointed.

- **$40,000 in Sales generated for a book** that had been sitting idle on Amazon before

> *With the right tools YOU too can turn your business around*

My Story

we started working with the author/chiropractor.

- **15% increase in Sales** for the main distributor of promotional materials, who already had 50% market share.

Over the past three years, I have personally helped more than 100 companies achieve massive growth. Some companies increased Sales by 30% within the first month of working with us; others tripled their Sales within a year.

I put all the knowledge I gathered – and much more – into what is today known as **Business Lens™**, a toolkit to identify what business owners don't do well or enough of in their company. This is **a tool that reveals the naked truth about any business**. It measures, mathematically, the gap between your company and Best Practices. The bigger the gap, the more growth potential the company has. Plus, it shows business owners where they need to focus to maximize Sales and profits.

This was the start of Tooliers, the platform with Smart Business solutions for small enterprises to increase profitability and become leaders in their niche. We now have clients around the globe and what's most important is not that we are making money, but that we help those who need us and our tools to smarten their businesses and achieve bigger profits faster.

Above all, I am proud of having built something that lasts beyond me. I know people will benefit from my current activities even after I am no longer here.

What's really in it for me? Or you?

> *When you focus on the right things in your business, you have the recipe to success*

My Story

FREEDOM!

The freedom to do what I want, when I want; to live anywhere in the world… and most importantly to be ME!

> *So what does this have to do with you and your business?*

You too can have the FREEDOM you want!

And I guess this is one reason you are reading this – you know you can do more and you want to.

The economy changes rapidly these days. As a small business owner, it is easy to run your business as if lost in a dark forest, thinking only of *survival*. You might forget about the destination. You are most likely involved with paying the next bill, dealing with a crisis after your best employee has left, trying to make up for that lost customer, deciding what kind of paper to buy for the copy machine and many other activities that keep you 'busy' and working hard.

But do you work *smart*? What if there was **a better way to achieve those dreams** you had when you started your business?

One third of business owners **want to grow their businesses, but don't know how and where to start**. The rest would like to maintain their business. The reality, however, is that 80% of businesses fail in the first five years and 96% in the first 10 years (this according to Michael Gerber, author of The *E-Myth*).

These facts also inspired me to write this book. I want to help YOU, a business owner, to *enjoy* your entrepreneurship. I want to help driven entrepreneurs just like you to achieve the success you deserve.

Business Unlimited is a collection of Best Practices I have seen and learned during my 20-year career in professional services. I learned about these tactics from seminars, workshops, conferences and summits,

My Story

and I have tried and tested them on my business and on our clients' businesses. When you master the tactics that follow, you will be able to compete with multinational companies, with Fortune 500 companies, as their equal. Because you know what? They use exactly the same tactics you are about to discover.

This book is part of my mission to empower 1,000,000 entrepreneurs to change the world while they achieve their personal and professional objectives fast, with ease.

Happy reading and enjoy the transformation of your business!

Ozana

Your Smarter Profits Accelerator

P.S. If you are serious about growing your Sales and profits, raising your profile and helping way more people, I invite you to join any of my online or live Master Classes and bootcamps.

Visit My Events Page *(www.ozanagiusca.com/my-events)* to get the updated schedule of my events and register to those most suitable for you.

Why have I written this book?

I wrote this book because I believe YOU can achieve much more especially in today's economy, which is the best possible environment for driven entrepreneurs and small businesses to really take off and finally get to the next level, especially because of the Internet and technology developments.

I believe that small businesses are changing the world and making it a better place... provided they deploy the right systems. Thus, this book is about a systematic approach to business so you achieve your dreams and gain the respect you deserve.

Turning around my own company from the brink of bankruptcy in 2008 to a business selling on all continents was an incredible journey. Having been through 3 years with no sales (before Tooliers took off), I made every possible mistake. I also realised that business can be fun. So I made it my mission to empower 1,000,000 entrepreneurs to make a bigger impact, by proving them with full clarity on their business, and, of course, the right tools. Bottom line, I want to reduce the entrepreneurial struggle by encouraging small business owners and experts to first think strategically and then implement any tactic they consider. This way, they finally get results quickly with no stress or overwhelm.

This book is about sharing some of the lessons we've learnt so you build a profitable business and unleash your unlimited potential... **hence BUSINESS UNLIMITED**.

You hear me talk about Smart Business, which is the vehicle to get there... A Smart Business is flexible in approach, leverages what you have and know, and systematically attracts clients online so you scale and grow exponentially. This, of course, enables you, its founder and commander, to be anywhere you want, and not chained to your desk 16 hours per day.

My Story

Regardless of being early stage or a successful entrepreneur, if you are driven to achieve more, to create more value, to serve more people and improve their lives while you get what you want, then I would love to support you in your journey.

Let's change the world together!

Introduction

How to use this book

You don't have to start with Tactic 1, or to read this collection chronologically. Start with the tactic that feels the most interesting to you. Each tactic addresses a different Stage of a business. You may find one tactic more relevant than another. Read the relevant ones first and feel free to jump from one tactic to another.

You will see that each of the 101 Tactics concludes with a short exercise that will make it easy to apply the tactic to your business. If you are serious about growing your business, it is essential that you *decide how to apply* the tactic you have just read and *do the exercises* that follow. While doing the exercises, write down whatever comes to mind.

Don't get overwhelmed by all the information in this book. You don't have to use it all at once. However, you will be surprised by how much of this book applies to you and your business. Take the knowledge on board, and don't get desperate if you can't find a way of using it on the spot. The more you practice using these tactics, the more ideas you will get – in time you may even find ways to use those tactics you thought were not relevant to your business.

Revisit the book as your business Needs and Goals change. Reread certain tactics, or tackle new ones. This book may well become your 'Bible for a Smarter Business'.

Introduction

The finer details

Definitions of all words or terms that appear in ***bold and italics*** or starting with Caps can be found in the Glossary of Terms.

I use **customer** as a generic term. In your industry, you may prefer the word client, visitor, guest, user, or patient, for example.

I use examples from **a range of industries**. Feel free to adapt and apply the tactics to your own business.

Throughout the book, I use **products** and **services** interchangeably. Note, however, that an **offering** is not the same as a product or service. For our purposes, an offering refers to the product or service combined with its price, packaging and positioning. So, product X as offering A is sold for $100 as a stand-alone product. Product X could also be packaged as offering B, which includes another item or addresses a different market or just has a different packaging, and sells for $200.

Example:

> *Cashew nuts can be sold in large quantities (tons) to wholesalers, who then repackage the nuts in smaller quantities (say 1 kilogram) to be sold at the market. Those same cashew nuts can be sold in supermarkets in packs of 300 grams; these look more attractive and command a higher price. Or the cashew nuts can be sold per 100 grams in a high-end bar, for a premium price.*
>
> *The product is the same – cashew nuts – but with different packaging and/or positioning, it becomes a different offering and commands a different price.*
>
> *The target market could be the same or different. I could be buying a 1 kg pack at the market, but I could also buy the 300 gram packs in gas stations.*

Introducing Tooliers®

Tooliers® (www.tooliers.com) is THE latform with high-end business growth solutions to empower entrepreneurs to build their SMART business so they increase profitability, reduce struggle and become leaders in their niche.

Business Lens™ is the digital mirror of your business. It shows you the naked truth about your business. It shows your unrealized growth potential.

Business Lens™ Diagnosis is the process of using Business Lens™ to perform a full analysis of your business, which identifies the areas that need more of your attention so you take your business to the next level.

Business Doctor is one of our growth programs, where we perform the Business Lens™ Diagnosis, and issue suggestions and recommendations for tactics and strategies to execute, so you grow your business immediately as well as long term.

Businesses don't grow unless people grow. You rock! By reading this book, you are enabling personal growth together with business growth!

Bonus:
Steady Growth -
Systematize Your Business

Tactic #1

Follow a System

> *Focus your efforts exactly where they are required as your business grows*

I have created the **Business Growth Focus Formula** (see below) because so often I see business owners focusing on the wrong things. You want to do what you like to do, or what you are best at and this is fine to a certain extent. But if you want to have a *highly successful business*, you need to approach it systematically, and change Focus according to which Stage your business is at. Focus doesn't mean you only work on a certain area of your business or that you do it all by yourself. It means you **concentrate your efforts on a particular area of your business at a particular time.** It also means that you learn more about that area. Of course, you can involve Experts and you can Delegate, as long as this area is where your mind is. Even if you outsource, you inevitably acquire more knowledge in that area.

> *Be disciplined and Focus on what you have to in order to reach your Objectives and fulfill your dreams*

The idea is simple: your Focus, as the owner of the business, moves from 'Sales' to 'Sources and Resources' to 'Systems', as your company grows. This is the **best business growth strategy**. Focusing on one part of the business does not mean that you *only* deal with that part. It means, say, that you allocate half of your time to it, while the other half is split between anything else you would normally deal with. Above all, you, as the business owner, must focus on what needs your Focus, even if it is not necessarily what you *like* doing.

Let's talk about each area of a business:

Business Growth Focus Formula

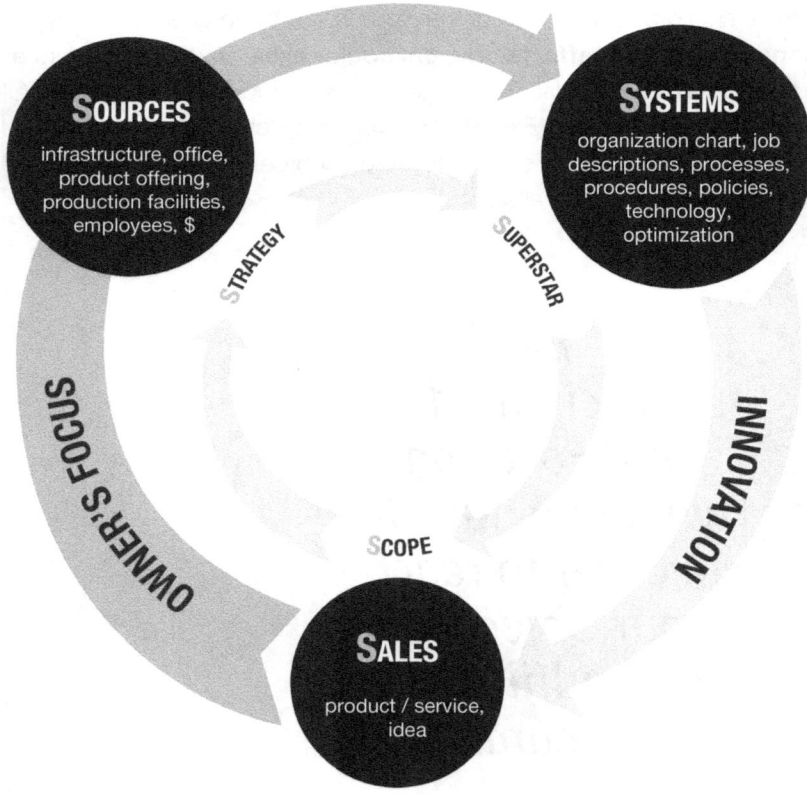

1 Focus on Sales

When you are at the beginning with your business, or when you launch a new product or open a new location. 'Sales' is split into two parts:

(i) selling your product or service;

(ii) selling your idea.

Selling your product or service is what you would generally understand as: giving your product / service to your customer in exchange for money (the price paid).

Selling your idea means getting people to buy into what you are doing. To share your dream, your vision and to get others excited about it. Selling your idea to current employees, potential employees, partners, suppliers, banks and any other person who is necessary to run the business smoothly, is as important as selling your product. You cannot create a business on your own. To achieve your Objectives, you need people around you. And those people don't join just because you think they should. It is tempting to believe they see and understand as you do, but they don't. You have to give them reasons to opt in, just as you give reasons to your customers to buy your product.

During this Stage, you have only a **Scope**. You know where you want to get to, but it is still flexible. You need the market reaction and partners' Feedback in order to ensure you have the right product, the right offering, both for your *customers* and for your business partners. The offering for the *customer* is a widely used concept: 'Buy this product for this price because it solves this problem in this way.' The offer for *business partners* sounds something like this: 'Bring customers to our business and you get x% from all the money they spend with us.' This is how you have to think of the Value proposition for your customers and your business partners. All parties have to win. And everything has to make sense and be clear from the outset.

② Focus on Sources and Resources

Once your product or service sells by itself; in other words, when customers buy your product or service without you having to convince each of them individually. By 'Sources' I mean everything that enables you to deliver to your customer; that is, your overall infrastructure: production facility, office space, logistics, as well as your employees and money to buy raw materials and invest in further growth. No point selling if you can't deliver, right?

When you have gotten to this phase, **you have a Strategy in place.** Now that you know what and how you sell, and for how much, you can create Specific Objectives and a clear path to achieving them.

3 Focus on System

When you are confident that you have a product that sells and that you can deliver and satisfy your customer. By 'Systems', I mean organizational charts, job descriptions, processes, procedures, policies, IT system, and potentially CRM / ERP (software to help with planning and managing your Resources and your customers).

In this phase you **consolidate what you have**; you organize things internally and clean up your mess. By this Stage, you and your staff have tried various ways of producing and delivering Value and you now know who does what in your company, and how. It is therefore time to document everything that is happening in your company, to put order in place. This helps you and your current employees to better understand how things are being done in your company and to become more efficient. Having these Systems in place also makes for an easier and more efficient process when you bring new people into your organization. You have 'machinery' that works, effectively and efficiently.

What you care about now is **becoming a Superstar Company**. By 'Superstar', I mean being the best in your niche. If you think of your industry as a pyramid, there is only one company on top, a few on the second layer, then the third, and so on... until the bottom, where you find plenty of companies. Your Objective is to **get as close as possible to the top**. Why? Because if anything destructive happens in the economy or in your industry, or if anything happens that can adversely affect your business, you hardly feel it if you are on top. The financial crisis in 2008 resulted in many companies going bankrupt or being close to bankrupt – this is because they were at the bottom of the pyramid in their niche. If a tsunami comes, or the state does construction on the road in front of your shop or office, you need to be in such a strong position that your business does not suffer. This is being a Superstar Company.

After Systems are in place, you need to focus on **Innovation** if you want to take your company to the next level, in which case you go back to Sales in another growth cycle. Alternatively, you retire or sell your company (or you leave it as is and continue to manage 'in the business', which may eventually go downhill).

> *Shift Focus as your company develops and grows*

TAKE ACTION NOW!

Based on the Stage of your business development, decide which of the three areas discussed above requires your Focus. Write it down:

_____
_____
_____
_____
_____

What are your biggest current Challenges? Write these here; then use the tactics in this book to find ways of overcoming these Challenges.

Challenge 1:
_____
_____

Challenge 2:
_____
_____

Challenge 3:
_____
_____

Challenge 4:
_____
_____

Challenge 5:
_____
_____

Increase Internal Efficiency

Tactic #32

Automate Processes

> *When you repeat a task five times or more, you need to think about Automating it*

Initially, when you set up your company, you did the Sales, the customer delivery and took the trash out. Then you employed a few people and trained them to do things the way you did. You are not a one-man show anymore; you own and run a business. But what happens when an employee leaves? Well, you recruit another person – who you have to train. But what if you have no time to train them, if you have taken on other responsibilities that keep you busy? Is it not better to **have processes and procedures in place** so that new recruits can easily learn (by themselves or with minimal assistance) how to do their job?

So you have put processes in place. Now take this one step further… Is it not even better to Automate these processes; that is, to facilitate the process being carried out independently, by itself? (For more information on getting Technology to revolutionize your organizational processes, see Tactic #100 'Leverage with Technology'.)

This is how it's done!

Let's take invoicing as an example. You invoice a client every quarter. Initially you remember when to send the invoice out – it's your first contract, so how can you forget? Later, as you acquire more contracts, you might have someone in your company capture all contracts into an Excel spreadsheet to check and update regularly for you. But instead you could be using software that programs these invoices to be issued automatically. Better still, this software will ensure invoices are also sent to the client automatically and registered in your accounts.

Save time and costs by using Technology

TAKE ACTION NOW!

Write down 5 actions that you (or your staff) perform five times or more:
1. _____
2. _____
3. _____
4. _____
5. _____

For each action, think of at least 2 ways you could Automate it:
Action 1:
1. _____

2. _____

Action 2:
1. _____

2. _____

Action 3:
1. _____

2. _____

Action 4:
1. _____

2. _____

Action 5:
1. _____

2. _____

Tactic #33

Plan the Day

This is equally valid for both you and your staff. Everyone in your company should plan each day.

But what about all those things that have to be done on the spot and cannot be anticipated? No problem: when you break down your day into tasks, you plan for miscellaneous activities too.

You are in control of your work and your time, and you need to schedule in those things you want to accomplish. Otherwise you will end up answering the phone, discussing something with an employee by the coffee machine, or fighting fires. If you don't know when you will be working on specific tasks, other things will always come along that 'need to be solved urgently'. And you will never have the time to work on the tasks that are most important to you.

> *Are you sure you are talking to the right person?*

If about one third of your personal assistant's day cannot be planned in advance, then they will plan the other two thirds and leave the remaining time open for on-the-spot tasks.

Put it into practice!

> Good planning also involves allocating big things that take a long time into small chunks of time. (See Tactic #36 'Be Efficient with Your Time' for more on Chunking Up and Down.) In other words, break tasks that take a long time into smaller pieces that can be dealt with regularly. For example, I allocated one day per week to write this book, because I wanted to have it ready in four months.

Divide big projects into small, manageable chunks to be dealt with over time

If your employees don't plan their day, you will never be completely satisfied with their performance. When you ask someone to do something for you, two possibilities emerge:

1. They drop everything else to do your task, in which case something else that was important will not be accomplished.
2. They carry on with their work until it is finished (if ever), before moving on to your request.

Which outcome do you prefer? I would say neither! With careful planning, your staff can follow through on their responsibilities and on your task in due time.

Increase Internal Efficiency

TAKE ACTION NOW!

Write down the most 5 important things you have to deal with. 'Important' refers to those tasks that make a difference in your business and not what is urgent. Put them in order of importance. For each action, estimate how much time you need to complete it.

1. _____
_____
Time required: _____

2. _____
_____
Time required: _____

3. _____
_____
Time required: _____

4. _____
_____
Time required: _____

5. _____
_____
Time required: _____

Increase Internal Efficiency

If any of the tasks / actions above take more than 10 hours for you or your staff to complete, break them down into manageable steps below.

Step 1. _____
_____

Step 2. _____
_____

Step 3. _____
_____

Step 4. _____
_____

Step 5. _____
_____

Insert the above tasks / actions – including each step to completion – into your diary and stick to them. Treat these tasks as important meetings that you cannot miss – even when the task involves working by yourself.

Tactic #34

Use Meetings

I say *use* meetings and not have meetings because the Goal is to train everyone in your company to save issues to be discussed with the boss for scheduled meetings. The only exception to this rule is any issues that truly are urgent. **Issues that are not urgent should be put on a list and dealt with in one go during a meeting.** This tactic helps both you to and your managers have a more productive day.

If you have employees or colleagues coming into your office all the time – to ask you to sign a document, to authorize a payment, or to seek your opinion – you are constantly interrupted. To avoid this, schedule set times for these discussions. For example, your accounts person may come to you to authorize payments every day at 10 am and *not* three times a day (or whenever she feels like it). Or your product manager may come to you to discuss progress every day at 11 am and *not* every half hour (or every time he has a question or problem).

As for those urgent issues that can't be predicted, allocate an hour per day in which you take 'got a minute' meetings. So if anyone in the company has a challenge during the day, they know that your door is open between 3 and 4 pm to talk about such issues.

Find Strategic Solutions to problems

It is also a waste of time if the same kinds of problems or issues are being discussed at these meetings. Find a Solution that puts an end to the issue; solve it for good. For example, if it is the third time that you find an employee stealing from your company, it is not enough to fire that employee. You need to put in place a System to prevent this happening again. Your reaction and solution should also be made clear in a public announcement to your company, so no one will even *think* of stealing from your company in future.

Increase Internal Efficiency

Apply these good practices to manage your time more efficiently, but also train your managers to do the same – and you will *all* be more productive.

TAKE ACTION NOW!

List 10 actions you were asked to do by your staff in the past couple of days. Be sure to include requests that interrupted your work on other, important tasks. Once you have identified these issues, you can deal with them collectively during meetings rather than on an ad-hoc basis.

1. _____

2. _____

3. _____

4. _____

5. _____

6. _____

7. _____

8. _____

9. _____

10. _____

Tactic #35

Increase Internal Efficiency

Use an Agenda at Meetings

You probably have a lot of meetings – but do you achieve what you want to in those meetings? In fact, do you even know what you want to achieve from each meeting?

> *Make a habit of setting up your Objectives and an Agenda for each meeting*

Setting an Agenda for each meeting is crucial, because everyone needs to know what the meeting is about. And more importantly, the person calling the meeting needs to know exactly what the meeting is about, because otherwise you may end up having a meeting for the sake of having a meeting, without discussing anything useful. Without an Agenda, you could end up discussing all sorts of other unrelated subjects, which are not important, and don't really help the organization.

Increase Internal Efficiency

The Agenda keeps everyone focused and ensures everything important is covered.

Encourage your colleagues to set their Objectives too. You don't have to be there to have them follow good practices. Everyone in your organization should approach meetings with maximum efficiency. Otherwise, they are better off going for a drink, or taking a walk in the park!

An Agenda is good when you know the Objective of the meeting, the subjects you want to talk about, and how much time is allocated to each subject matter. Appoint someone to keep track of this and make sure you cover everything on the Agenda during the available time frame.

Go one step further and follow these simple yet powerful techniques in your meetings:

- **Take minutes.** Appoint one person who is responsible for recording the minutes of the meeting and for circulating this to all participants and other stakeholders (if applicable). The minutes should include the main subjects discussed and, most importantly, actions agreed upon: who does what by when. If, like me, you have a bad memory, you need something in writing to refer to after the meeting. This must be detailed enough to jog your memory. Also, anyone who missed the meeting, but is interested in the subject, should be able to understand what was discussed from the minutes.

- **Assign tasks.** There is no point writing in the minutes what was discussed if tasks are not assigned. All participants should have clarity on what they and others are responsible for after the meeting. Our minutes look like this: 'New campaign to our prospects interested in increased efficiency. VL to draft a message that informs them about our new tool on increasing personal efficiency. AV to send the message...' and so on.

- **Assign deadlines.** Each task has to have a time frame. Let's say you assign someone to prepare a presentation for the next client meeting. Ensure you have clarity on when the meeting is, and by when the person responsible is expected to finalize the presentation. Have interim deadlines if Feedback needs to be given by other members

of the team. Our minutes would look something like this: 'IV to draft presentation by 22 March, OG to provide Feedback by 25 March, IV to finalize by 28 March.'

- **Assign follow-up actions.** Often you discuss various issues during your meeting and generate great ideas that you may want to implement. And then what happens? Nothing! This is why follow-up actions have to be assigned – then you know who needs to do what by when, and those people are held responsible for completing their tasks. For example: 'DC in charge of building a video campaign. He will research options to embed videos in our website, and recommend solution by 5 Apr. Campaign to be ready by 27 Apr.'

- **Monitor progress.** You have assigned responsibilities – with deadlines – and you now need to ensure people take action on their responsibilities. Appoint someone to be in charge of checking on progress, to ensure the team members are doing what they are supposed to do. Also refer to Tactic #41 'Get a Reporting System in Place'.

Systematic approach ensures success in business

Increase Internal Efficiency

TAKE ACTION NOW!

Note down the next 3 meetings you have scheduled. Write the subject(s) of each meeting and with whom they are taking place.

1. _____
_____
_____

2. _____
_____
_____

3. _____
_____
_____

For each meeting, write down 5 items to be included in the Agenda.

Meeting 1:
1. _____

2. _____

3. _____

4. _____

5. _____

Meeting 2:

1. _____

2. _____

Increase Internal Efficiency

3. _____

4. _____

5. _____

Meeting 3:

1. _____

2. _____

3. _____

4. _____

5. _____

Tactic #36

Increase Internal Efficiency

Be Efficient with Your Time

Chunk Up and Chunk Down your activities

Most business people are busy. They are busy because they either like to be busy as it makes them feel important, or because they don't know any other way. The model below shows you how to accomplish much more within the same time frame. **Time is your most precious Resource, and it should be used wisely.**

Chunking refers to breaking an activity into pieces ('chunks'). You *Chunk Up* or you *Chunk Down* depending on how known or unknown the task is to you or someone else in your team and how comfortable you feel with that task, to be dealt with by someone else. By Chunking Up things you or others know, you free up brain space. You also Delegate as a 'chunk' and have fewer responsibilities.

Chunking Down: you've seen it in action before!

> When you learnt how to drive, your instructor told you to open the car door, to insert the key into the contact, to look in the rear-view mirror, to signal, press the clutch, then the accelerator and go. 'Driving' was broken down into small pieces that you could handle. Imagine how you would have reacted had someone given you the car key and said, 'Drive!' You would have felt overwhelmed, and refused. Your instructor, by Chunking Down, made it possible – and eventually easy – for you to drive. Now that you know how to drive, driving is, well, just driving.

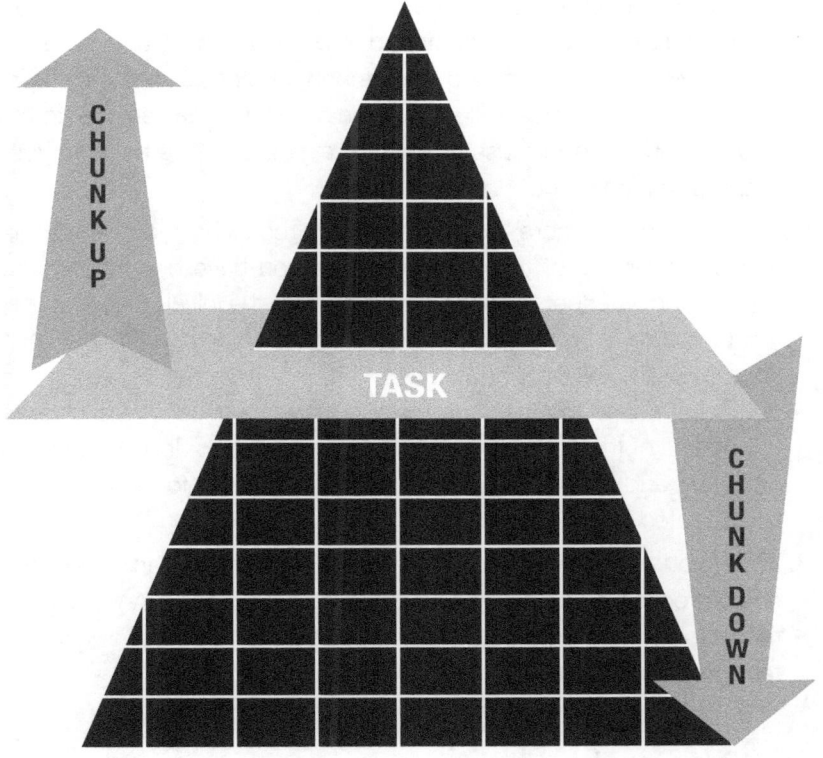

By Chunking Down the unknown, you make it easy for yourself to deal with that one task. You break it down into manageable pieces, which you can deal with, rather than postponing or procrastinating because you don't know how to start and how to handle it.

But how does Chunking Up apply in the workplace? Let's look at recruitment:

1. When you recruited your first employee, you had to publish the advertisement (after drafting the Job Description), receive CVs, read the CVs, select the ones you found appropriate, call candidates for an interview, meet them and understand whether or not they were the right fit, make notes, reflect, make a decision, make an offer to the chosen candidate, discuss again, and eventually have her sign your employment contract.
2. As you become more experienced with recruiting, you can begin to Delegate parts of this process. Once you have drafted the Job Description, your personal assistant might do the initial stages so that you become involved again later when you meet the candidates. Then your PA drafts the offer and deals with the new recruit. By doing this you have moved the task from being totally Chunked Down towards the middle of the scale, where your role is limited to Job Description, interview, and final decision; i.e. only three 'chunks' for you. The rest is Delegated to your assistant.
3. When you have someone else in the company that can handle the entire process (let's call her Anca), your task becomes: 'Anca, please recruit one more Business Doctor Consultant'. You have just one task. You have Chunked it all the way Up!

> *By Chunking Up things you know, you free up brain space, as they become one activity that eventually gets Delegated to others*

TAKE ACTION NOW!

Write down 3 activities with which you are familiar and which you could Chunk Up:

1. _____
_____
_____

2. _____
_____
_____

3. _____
_____
_____

4. Write down 3 activities you find difficult to deal with. Each of these activities can then be Chunked Down.

1. _____
_____
_____

2. _____
_____
_____

3. _____
_____
_____

Now identify a person within your company to whom you can Delegate each of the above activities.

Tactic #37 — Increase Internal Efficiency

Strengthen the Weakest Link

Fix the crack, not the leak!
Your business is only as strong as its Weakest Link

The strength of any System depends on its weakest component. In a business, that may be an employee, a procedure, a process, a System, an activity... **The Weakest Link is the area or individual with the lowest level of performance.**

A few years ago, I was heading home from the seaside in my BMW. Just 20 kilometers into the journey, I noticed a red light on the dashboard, indicating the car was over-heating (my 'leak'). I realized the radiator seal had broken (the 'crack'), which meant the engine would no longer

cool off and driving was too risky. The fact that the car was brand new, had good acceleration, good suspension (and good everything else) did not matter. The car could not do the job it was meant to do. I could not get home. I could not reach my destination. In the end, a tow truck took my car and me back to Bucharest; i.e. I moved to 'another company' to satisfy my need to get home. Of course, had I taken the car for a service before my trip, I would have known the radiator seal was broken. I would have replaced it and reached my destination in the manner planned.

Imagine your business is a car. If one part of the organization (one link) doesn't work as it should, and your whole organization does not reach its destination as a result, you have failed to meet your Objectives. Your Weakest Link is holding you back from achieving what you want.

> *The key is to identify the real Weakest Link – and fix it*

In the context of an organization, the Weakest Link could be one employee who does not deliver and causes delays in delivering your product to the customer. Or the Weakest Link could be a procedure that doesn't work, or a function that is not structured well enough to deliver Value.

Apply this tactic to your business!

You have a really great product, yet your Sales are low because you simply don't know how to sell. Your Sales function is your Weakest Link. Or the contrary: you sell a lot, but your clients are not happy, because you are not able to deliver appropriately. This is because you don't have the System or the people in place to deliver according to your promises.

Whatever it is, you need to fix the Weakest Link. Then you identify the next Weakest Link, and so on. Although there is always room for improvement, don't work on improving what you are already doing well. If you sell a lot but can't deliver, it doesn't make any sense to hire more salespeople. You need to address the delivery function, as *This* is bringing down your performance. This is precisely why, in our Tooliers® Diagnostic Reports, we invite clients to work on the dimension with the lowest score – this is the Weakest Link of the areas analyzed.

TAKE ACTION NOW!

Write down the 5 Weakest Links in your business and at least one possible Solution for each:

1. _____
_____
_____

2. _____
_____
_____

3. _____
_____
_____

4. _____
_____
_____

5. _____
_____
_____

Tactic #38

Increase Internal Efficiency

Eliminate Wasting Time in Routine Tasks

Touch issues once only

Touching an Issue refers to each time you 'visit' the issue before solving it. When an email is received, it may be opened to read, opened again to save the document attached, again to forward it, then to answer it and perhaps once more to file it. This is 'Touching' that issue *five times*.

Ideally an issue should be touched only once before it is solved.

Here's how not to do it!

> *After being involved in a car accident in Romania, the other party and I went to the police station to report the incident. The police officer accompanied us outside to look at the two damaged cars, before we went back inside to sort out the paperwork. First he asked for our driver's licenses and car papers. He took one driver's license, looked at it, put in on his desk. He took the other license, looked at it, put it on his desk. Then he went to fetch the relevant documents. Next he took my declaration, then the other driver's declaration. Then he looked again at my license, and again at the other license.*
>
> *He then went to get a paper clip to hold together his three documents. On his return, he looked at each driving license again. Then he took my declaration again. Then he took the other driver's declaration again. Eventually he took my license again to copy information to his document and did the same for the other driver. After more of the same, we went outside again, this time for him to take photos of the cars. Back inside, he looked again at our licenses and... you get my point.*

It took him over an hour to fill in the forms; it could have been done in five minutes. Go back and count how many times he touched our papers. If he had touched each paper once, the entire process would have been over quickly.

Why waste an hour on something you can do in five minutes? If the police officer in the example above had taken five minutes, he could have dealt with 11 more cases by the end of that hour. Instead he preferred to make others wait a few hours before he started dealing with them. Maybe that made him feel important, but, as a business owner, you want to be efficient. Your importance comes from you being able to achieve the results you want, not from being busy. And the same goes for your team.

Access everything in MAX five clicks

Have all your documents stored in your computer such that any document is within a maximum of five clicks away. Why would you want to waste time on opening loads of folders over and over again?

Throw issues away!

Throwing Issues Away means getting rid of issues that are of no importance; issues that are irrelevant or make no difference to the results you are after.

These tactics are valid for your entire company – not just for you alone.

Here's how it's done!

You drafted an internal document to be used for one meeting and never to be referred to again. Do you want to spend half a day putting your nice logo and branding on that document, or would like to you skip this, and just get the information down, circulate it and move on? You 'Throw Away' the unnecessary work on this document, as it does not make any difference to your results.

TAKE ACTION NOW!

Write down the 5 Weakest Links in your business and at least one possible Solution for each:

1. _____
_____
_____

2. _____
_____
_____

3. _____
_____
_____

4. _____
_____
_____

5. _____
_____
_____

Tactic #39

Increase Internal Efficiency

Get Used to Delegating

You already know that by Delegating you save time, achieve more, and grow your professional and business Value. You can multiply your results many times over once you start Delegating. You also know you can't do everything by yourself, for two reasons: you don't have the time to do everything and you don't always have the relevant skills or abilities.

Your time is your most precious commodity. Think how much you could do if you quadrupled your time. Well, you have the Resources: your employees. It is time to start Delegating.

> *Make sure each job is being done by the person most qualified to do it. If necessary, bring someone in*

Divide and conquer! Identify the tasks that others within your company can do as well as you. These are often routine tasks that do not require high-level skills or tasks that can be accomplished by someone else in your team.

Apply this to your business too!

> As a consultant, I was often preparing business plans for our clients. Today I have trained different people to (i) write those plans and (ii) develop the financial model and forecast the financial results. For a while I had to review their tasks. Today they have made such progress that I do not bring any more value by revising their work.
>
> As a business owner, I used to buy the office supplies myself, so that I could be sure of buying what I liked. I have since learnt to allow the driver to do the shopping. Who cares if the toilet paper is blue or yellow? I have learnt to notbe so particular so that I can concentrate on those things that matter for the business's growth.

Increase Internal Efficiency

By Delegating routine work you will have both less stress and more time to do work that matters the most. Having extra time will enable you to take on more challenging tasks and grow both as a leader and as a professional.

If you don't Delegate, you have to accept that your hourly rate will essentially be that of the person who can do the job. If you buy your own office supplies, you are then worth $10 per hour – or whatever you could pay someone else to do that job.

Make it work for you!

> If you were a construction company owner, would you rather:
> - come up with the engineering plan for a five-story building, build the foundation, carry the bricks and take the trash out for the next three years, or
> - hire an engineer to come up with the plan, build a team, assign responsibilities, hold people Accountable for results and have the whole building finished within three months? Engineer – to come up with the plan, bricklayers – to build the foundation, workers – to take the trash out... You know your skillset is beyond taking the trash out, right?

How many $10-an-hour jobs are you currently doing?

TAKE ACTION NOW!

List 10 actions you perform that would cost $10 per hour. Once you have identified them, get rid of them. Delegate these actions to people who cost less than you do.

1. _____

2. _____

3. _____

4. _____

5. _____

6. _____

7. _____

8. _____

9. _____

10. _____

Tactic #40

Increase Internal Efficiency

Give People the Right Tools When Delegating

It is your responsibility as the business owner to make it clear what you want, and to hold people responsible for what you want them to do. Focus on *results*. You want the job done, so this should matter to you.

People avoid taking on responsibility for various reasons. They may be afraid of failure, feel overwhelmed by the scope of the project, or just feel lazy. As their leader, you need to Motivate them, encourage them and ensure they can deliver according to your expectations. As soon as you became a leader (manager, boss, founder) you stopped being a regular employee. You are now a coach. Coaches must understand the importance of inspiring, teaching, and taking pride in teams attaining your Business Goals.

As a consultant, the number one thing I've learned is that entrepreneurs need to learn to Delegate. Do it efficiently and consistently. (See also Tactic #39 'Get Used to Delegating'.) Break down complex projects and plans into specific attainable tasks, assign those to your team members and hold them Accountable for the results – both meeting deadlines and quality of the work.

> *When you Delegate, tell people exactly what you expect from them, when their task is finished, and by when they have to finish it*

It is not enough to say: 'Do this for me.' You need to ensure your employee understands what they need to do and know how to go about it, by when they need to accomplish it and its importance. Are your employees making mistakes? Teach them. Losing Motivation? Delve into it: understand why; make corrections; cheer them up! Did your employees successfully reach their Goals? Share the victory and pride. They are your team.

Here's why you need to do this!

When we started Tooliers®, our online platform with business growth tools for small businesses, I asked one of my consultants to find an e-commerce (payment) solution for the project. Although we use the internet every day to buy things, none of us knows what a payment transaction really involves. I also told him to do this within a week, or we wouldn't be able to sell online; i.e. the reason, deadline and importance of the task were clear. But, two months later we still didn't have a payment solution in place. Why? Because he had to learn about online payments, to understand how the whole system works, to identify potential providers, to choose the best. This part was still relatively easy... next we had to apply for the payment processor to accept us. We even had to pay for our application to be considered. When we were rejected, we had to go back to square one and identify the next company we wanted to work with.

My colleague knew what he had to do and what result we required. However, because it was a completely new task, he could not deliver in time. I have to take responsibility for the mistake here, because I underestimated what the task involved.

> *When you want people to be responsible for their tasks, ensure you understand what it takes to accomplish that task, and assign a realistic time frame*

Increase Internal Efficiency

Be the coach for your staff

Increase Internal Efficiency

TAKE ACTION NOW!

Write down 5 actions you will take to improve the way you Delegate to ensure best delivery and as little involvement on your part as possible.

1. _____
_____
_____

2. _____
_____
_____

3. _____
_____
_____

4. _____
_____
_____

5. _____
_____
_____

Tactic #41   Increase Internal Efficiency

Get a Reporting System in Place

Ask staff to send Reports to their direct manager about progress made and tasks accomplished on a daily basis

A lot of people ask me how I manage my company when I spend so much of my time traveling and very few weeks of the year in the office with my staff. The answer is simple: I assign specific responsibilities to people and I hold them Accountable. But it is the *how* that is the key to this working. I ask all my staff to send me a Daily Report of what they have done. This is just a simple email, so they don't have to waste a lot of time on it, and contains what they have accomplished that day, what they need to do, any problems and proposed solutions, and where they seek my response.

The Reports follow this structure:

- **Tasks done.** This section includes only tasks that are totally finished and do not require further attention.
- **In progress.** This section includes tasks that have been started but not finished.
- **To do.** These are tasks that they have not started working on.

TASKS DONE	IN PROGRESS	TO DO
• _____	• _____	• _____
• _____	• _____	• _____
• _____		• _____

All tasks are prioritized and deadlines are assigned to each task. By doing this, I ensure my staff deal with the most important and urgent tasks first, rather than with whatever they like most. In addition, I know every day within minutes where they are and how they progressing – all I have to do is open a few emails.

Do it like this!

A consultant assigned to draft a Business Plan for a client would enter under To do: 'Business Plan for Client X. AB to do financials. Deadline 10 May.' This tells me that the consultant is fully responsible for the Business Plan, but uses AB (another consultant) to do the financial section. When the consultant starts working on the project, she will move the task to In progress. Here, she might write: 'Collected 60% of the info from client; intro and market section finished.' As she progresses, she will have completed more sub-sections. The task is moved to Done only after it has been delivered to the customer; i.e. not when it is done but still in her computer.

This tactic is a way to ensure everyone in the company delivers, as they know what they have to work on, and by when. These Reports include 'to do lists', which are useful both for me and for them. Whenever they have a new responsibility, they add it to their Report. This way, I know they are responsible for that task, and that they have assumed responsibility.

TAKE ACTION NOW!

Write down 5 actions that you will undertake to get a clearer picture of i) what is happening in your company (no matter where you are) and ii) at what stage various projects are. (Make sure your Reporting Systems are quick and efficient.)

1. _____
_____
_____

2. _____
_____
_____

3. _____
_____
_____

4. _____
_____
_____

5. _____
_____
_____

Measure Everything and Continuously Improve

> Don't obsess with finding the best or most accurate Performance Indicators in the world.
> Simply help your team continuously improve

You don't need complex KPIs (Key Performance Indicators) and sophisticated Performance Management Systems to review performance. If you have them, rather see KPIs as a way of being Accountable and of having your staff be Accountable – to ensure people deliver according to your expectations. KPIs or not, you do need to have enough controls in place to measure, track and, above all, encourage performance and efficiency at all levels within your company.

No matter how small or big your company, you need to consider some general principles when measuring performance and effectiveness. Start with your Strategic Objectives. For each major line of business, identify the most relevant indicators.

Putting it into practice!

Let's say my Objective is to achieve $1 million in online Sales in the next 12 months.

Q1: In the first quarter I am not concerned about the Sales at all. My Priority is to have the product offering perfect and the communication well set up. I could measure weekly how many email campaigns I have set up as well as how many social media followers I have. I am also interested in the number of people signing up for our newsletter and the number of people who express interest in our business by giving us their email address. Check www.ozanagiusca.com/60-sec-social-media-plan/ to create your Social Media Measuring Plan in 60 seconds or less by filling in 3 blanks (yes, it really is that simple).

Q2: In the next quarter, I want to see some Sales – say $10,000. The crucial indicator is now conversion on the site. How many emails do I need to send to get one sale? How much do I spend on Facebook ads compared to Google AdWords before making a sale? Each separate activity has to be measured to see which campaigns perform better. I could also look at how much time my employees spend on setting up a campaign and compare this to time required for sending messages on LinkedIn, which, although free, does require time. Bottom line: I want to know my Costs versus Sales for each Sales channel.

Q3: During the next quarter I am interested in improving conversions and in generating more traffic, so I look at the number of paying customers versus the total number of visitors. I also look at the best channels through which to bring visitors to the site.

Q4: It is only now that I am concerned about Sales and want to increase the Sale per marketing dollar spent.

You probably have different people doing different jobs, in which case you need to assess them against different indicators. Use Core Indicators (five to six core competencies common to the entire team), as well as Specific Indicators to account for the specifics of each job. Involve each person or team in choosing the right yardsticks.

I bet you use revenues or Sales to check whether you are on the right track. That's good, but not enough. Numerical indicators never tell the whole story (nor do technical skills). Good Sales are a strong indicator of an effective Sales force, but they show to a lesser extent how well your product developer did their job. Assign weights to the indicators (i.e. one indicator may count twice as much as another, because it is more important) and consider the most relevant ones for each job or function. If your salesperson is not that good with details, don't overreact. For them it is more important to follow-up on their leads, to be good negotiators,

Increase Internal Efficiency

and to close deals. Place a heavier weight on the most relevant skills or behaviors for each person… and also understand why things don't work as planned. That is, if the product doesn't have the characteristics that the market seeks, it is not the salesperson's fault, but that of the product development staff.

> *You can't afford to pay people who do not deliver. Nor can you afford to do their job*

In my opinion, for small businesses, Performance Management Systems (using KPIs) don't really matter that much. **You may be surprised to learn that Soft Skills and Organizational Culture can greatly impact the effectiveness and productivity of your team**. Continuous Feedback and an open Culture based on sharing the lessons learnt and guiding each other to improve can help more than the most sophisticated and expensive system in the world.

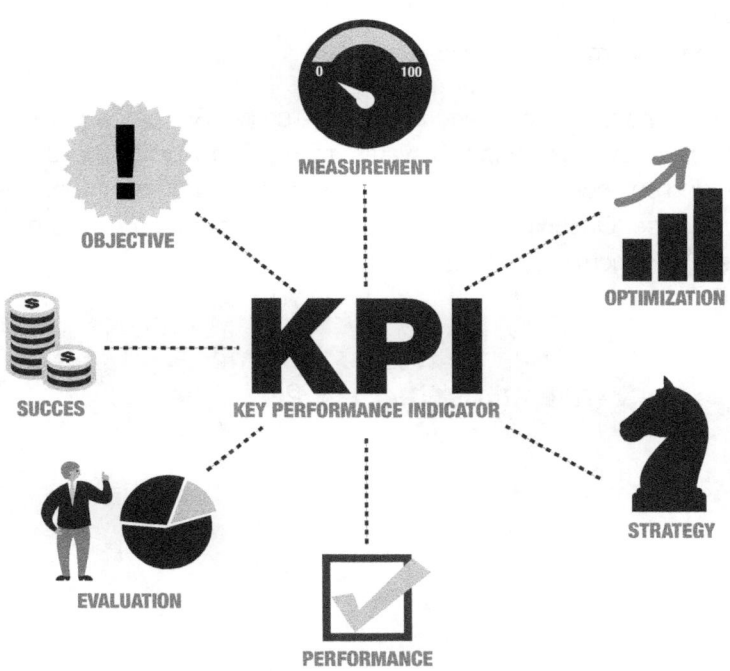

Soft Skills are hard to assess – and harder to do without. I challenge you to also consider the following when you assess the performance of your team:

- Consistently completing high-quality work on time
- Collaborating with each other to hit deadlines
- Persuading others to consider different points of view
- Appreciating the customer's perspective and his point of view
- Coaching and being coached on technical and non-technical matters
- Working successfully for a variety of managers, each with their own unique style
- Remaining flexible enough to handle rapidly changing requirements
- Making tough decisions with limited information and often dealing with ambiguity
- Challenging conventional wisdom and authority
- Helping team members who are struggling
- Taking over a project that's in trouble without being told to do so
- Managing multiple projects to a timeline
- Meeting budget restraints
- Prioritizing important tasks

Once you have a good Performance Evaluation System in place, shift your Focus towards using this system to *improve your business.* Focus your mind on how your employees can help each other to improve overall performance. Observe what the Best Performers do, and try to get the Worst Performers to do the same.

> *Get the Worst Performers to emulate the Best Performers*

TAKE ACTION NOW!

IIdentify 5 areas you would like to measure in the next year. For each area, write down how you will measure it:

1. _____
_____
_____

2. _____
_____
_____

3. _____
_____
_____

4. _____
_____
_____

5. _____
_____
_____

Tactic #43 — Increase Internal Efficiency

Have an Organizational Chart

An Organizational Chart clearly shows all the positions within the company, and the people in those positions. It also shows hierarchy and reporting lines. Everybody in the company needs to know their responsibilities, how they fit into the whole picture, and whom they need to work with.

You also need a Job Description for each employee. This document records the responsibilities of the employee, and a few other important factors. We have the following items in our Job Descriptions:

- Department
- Position
- Name
- Hierarchical relationship. Here we record the people he reports to, but also his subordinates.
- Backed-up by... If he is on holiday or absent for any reason, there should be a person on hand to do his job. This is important information, because this person has to know his job, and also has to be updated on what he has done, where things are at, and so on.
- Back-up for. He could be a back-up to one person for some types of responsibilities and to another person for other types of responsibilities.
- Approved by and agreed by [the person that drafted his Job Description, and the person whose Job Description it is]
- Signatures of both persons
- Duties and responsibilities. This area details what he is responsible for.
- Knowledge and skills required. This is mainly used when we recruit someone.

I would imagine things change continuously in your company. You acquire a new employee, you create a new department, or people take on more responsibilities. Be sure to update your Organizational Chart and Job Descriptions regularly. (I do this at least once a year.)

Increase Internal Efficiency

Consider involving your team in elaborating the Organizational Chart and Job Descriptions to increase job ownership.

> *Periodically upgrade your Organizational Chart and Job Descriptions*

TAKE ACTION NOW!

Write down when you last updated your Organizational Chart:
_____

Write down any changes since the last update:

1. _____

2. _____

3. _____

4. _____

5. _____

6. _____

7. _____

8. _____

9. _____

10. _____

Increase Internal Efficiency

Have a Consistency System in Place

You are a company, a unit. You want your people to perform in a particular, united way

Imagine your flight has been cancelled due to bad weather. The airport is a mess, because all other flights have been cancelled too. There are long queues at all counters. You manage to speak to someone working for your airline company and she tells you to go and make your own arrangements and that the airline company will reimburse your expenses. On your way out, you bump into another person working for the same airline company and check that you're doing the right thing. She tells you that if you make your own arrangements, you will not be reimbursed. What do you do? You get angry and feel even more frustrated. You consider going back to stand in line, but you've lost your place and would have to start at the back again.

Yes, this is a true story. It happened to me when I was flying from Vegas to Brussels, and London was a mess due to fog. Airline representatives were trying to get us out of the airport to reduce the chaos. The point, however, is that you don't want your customers to get conflicting responses from your staff. You want everyone who works for you to represent the company in an unswerving manner. **You want all your employees to perform each aspect of their job with a degree of excellence and Consistency.** You want to get predictable results, because Training and Skills are Consistent.

To create Consistency, you need to ensure that:

- Each supervisor and each employee would give a similar answer to a particular question or problem (both internal and external to the company).
- Client treatment is similar, regardless of who is dealing with the client.
- All staff members know what is considered good performance and attitude.

Business Unlimited

And there is something more...

You want to make sure that everyone in your company knows the company's vision, and its Brand Values.

What are Brand Values? These are about what is important for the company. The principles, the beliefs, the attitudes, the vision that they would never compromise on.

I feel obliged to write about Brand Values, because I see so many business owners concerned only about the money they make, without having a clear vision.

Most business owners are not clear about their Brand Values. They don't even think about them, and are unaware that they need to articulate them to their employees. Brand Values are so important because they determine certain behavior, especially when it comes to dealing with customers. They may determine the way the company reacts to bad publicity or even how to cope when an employee leaves. They also encourage teamwork, by uniting everyone working for the company.

TAKE ACTION NOW!

Write down 5 ideas you can implement in your company to improve Consistency:

1. _____
_____
_____

2. _____
_____
_____

3. _____
_____
_____

4. _____
_____
_____

5. _____
_____
_____

Increase Internal Efficiency

Increase Internal Efficiency

Business Unlimited

Smart Business System™

In my experience, which includes being responsible for increasing the profits of 100 companies over the past three years – in some cases doubling and even tripling profits – I've noticed that most people running a small business or working alone, face 7 main challenges to increasing sales.

Many believe their lack of further success is due to legislation, taxation, red tape, banks not lending or the government not helping small businesses, but the truth is there are 7 challenges that are within your control to overcome, which makes all the difference.

It is important to understand these challenges, to identify which ones you are facing and then to use the very best system to overcome your specific challenges.

Because I also faced these challenges, specifically when I was struggling to sell with Tooliers *(www.tooliers.com)*, I have developed the **Smarter Business System™**, which is our battle-tested solution for achieving objectives faster.

My team and I have been using this system on a daily basis. Initially we kept it for ourselves and for a select group of clients. Now, we share it freely with fellow entrepreneurs, experts and driven professionals who want more.

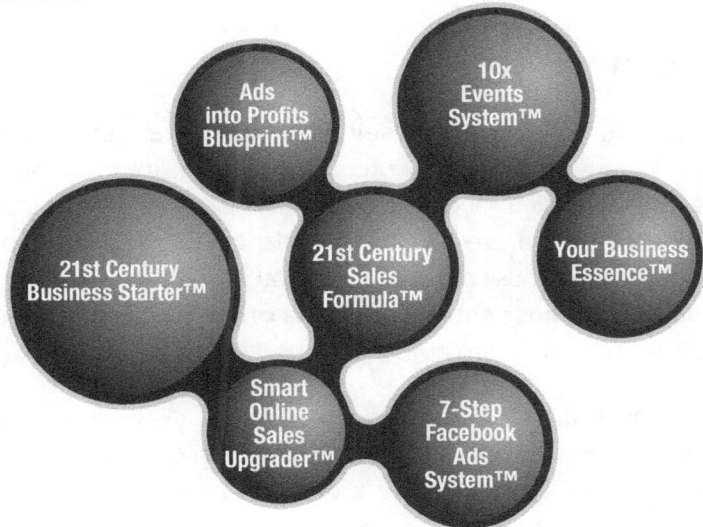

Smart Business System™

It is my pleasure to invite you to my online or live Master Classes in which I detail the system and its components.

Join me wherever it is convenient for you. Select from the events listed at **www.ozanagiusca.com/my-events** whatever best suits you and your needs. Some events are free and some require an investment.

Below I share more about the 7 challenges that block the growth of most businesses as well as the sub-system I have developed to overcome each challenge.

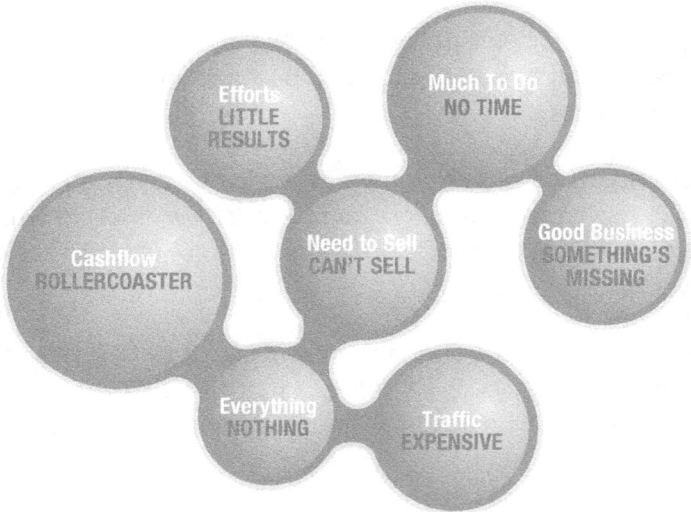

Challenge #1

Small business owners **want to sell more and have a stable, solid income**. Increasing the sales involves having a saleable product or service, a sales system and a way to feed this system with potential leads. Because there are various potential issues that need to be addressed before a business really takes off and grows exponentially, the **cash flow of most entrepreneurs is often like a rollercoaster** (sometimes up, more often down).

Too many meetings end up being a waste of time. Networking may be okay for social reasons, but few people buy from those they meet at events. A potential client suddenly goes cold... and whatever we do, it seems that people are simply no longer interested in buying.

Today, **people don't buy the way they used to**.

Due to the technology developments and the internet, the way people buy has changed. Which means that if you want to sell more, you also need to change your approach.

You need to adapt your business to the current reality. This is having the 21st Century Business Approach, the 21st Century Business Marketing Methods, and the 21st Century Business Essentials (this is not about the essentials in your business, which I am sure you have, but about the essentials that your business needs to give to you, its owner), because business as usual, as in the past, is no longer an option.

The key words here are Customer's Journey, a term that many experts talk about, but which is not understood and leveraged as it should be. This is about you **building a number of pre-programmed interactions with your potential clients, so you take them from "I don't know you" to buying from you and even recommending you to others**.

In most cases, such a 'journey' doesn't happen naturally. You need to engineer it, so your potential clients take the right steps (depending on where they are in relation to wanting your type of product or service) towards you and only you.

In order to build the road for such a journey, you need the 21st Century Business MAP.

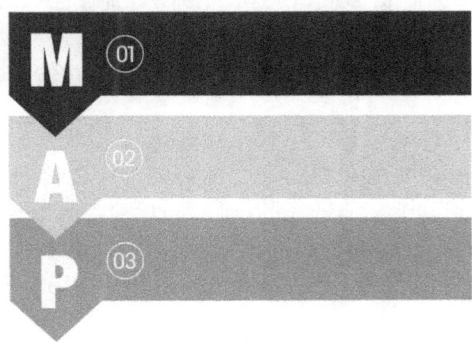

Smart Business System™

Deploying this system is the way to not only stay in business long term, but to thrive and generate increasing cash flow.

We are talking about combining online with offline activities, about talking to the potential client more but mainly in an automated or semi-automated manner, so you really leverage what you have and know so you achieve smarter profits faster.

I discuss this new approach and how to position your company, product or service and how to build your Customers' Journeys during the Smart Business Accelerator™ *(www.ozanagiusca.com/kim-en)*, strategic workshop over two days.

If you want to be in full control of your business; if you are fed up with trying various approaches which waste your money and time only to bring stress and frustration; and if you are committed now to investing to transform and scale your business, to maximize your profits and increase your impact so you achieve YOUR objectives, then I'm here to support you!

I invite you to join me for my next workshop where we will plan your Smarter Business *(www.ozanagiusca.com/kim-en)*.

Challenge #2

Before they started working with us, our clients were doing various activities, trying to sell to as many people as possible, but only getting a few clients.

I often see entrepreneurs busily developing a new product, serving existing clients, trying to source extra help, doing the admin tasks and even taking the trash out. They are constantly busy, feeling overwhelmed by how much they have to do… but what progress do they actually make?

For these entrepreneurs, I have developed the **Smart Online Sales Upgrader™**, to enable you to get more and better clients fast. Because generating business online can be done on auto or semi-auto pilot and when the system is deployed correctly, you have more time to do what you really love.

See in the illustration below how you can deploy this method to build your own system, to generate business online and have a constant and predictable cash flow.

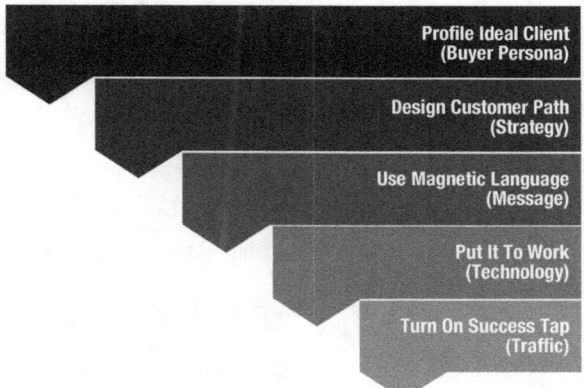

Under our guidance, participants in our Smart Online Sales Bootcamp™ *(www.ozanagiusca.com/sos-bootcamp-en)* achieve in two days what they have struggled to do on their own for years!

This method works because it has been tested on more than 400 entrepreneurs in most industries, ranging from professional services (consultants, coaches, experts) to manufacturing and retail.

The secret here is CLARITY. And to get clarity you need to go through a series of questions and, of course, answer them systematically, on paper.

Challenge #3

The majority of small businesses want more traffic in their store (online or offline) or visiting their website. Traffic is expensive, though, and they can't afford to waste resources on promotional activities that don't lead to sales.

We've figured that Facebook is the best platform right now to get traffic. It works for all businesses, but only when deployed correctly. If you are wondering if Facebook Ads are for you (i.e. investing in promotion on Facebook), join my next online Master Class *(www.ozanagiusca.com/facebook-ads-why-en)* on this subject.

Smart Business System™

We have developed the 7-Step Smart Business Facebook Ads System which we'll present during this Master Class. Simply go to **www.ozanagiusca.com/facebook-ads-system-en**, register, attend, take notes and implement.

We tested and tested… invested $100,000+ in our own campaigns and helped 300+ clients run profitable ads campaigns.

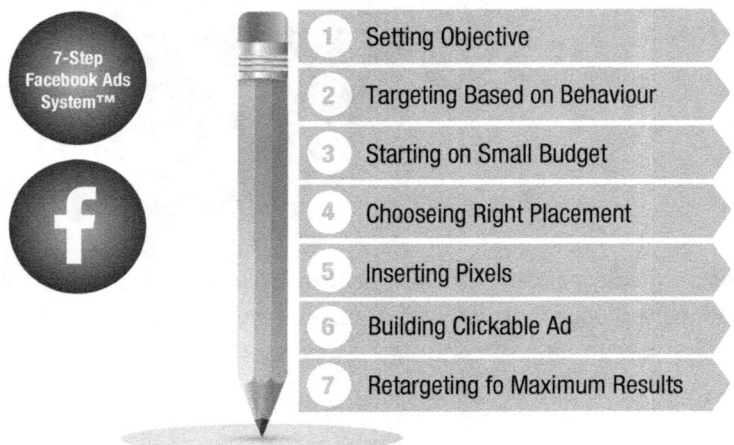

7-Step Facebook Ads System™

1. Setting Objective
2. Targeting Based on Behaviour
3. Starting on Small Budget
4. Chooseing Right Placement
5. Inserting Pixels
6. Building Clickable Ad
7. Retargeting fo Maximum Results

Challenge #4

Many people running their own show, be it a one-man venture or an established business, **need to sell but don't know how**. The truth is that selling is a skill you can learn. What's interesting is that most of our clients don't want to even consider taking sales courses. Because, just as they don't like others trying to sell to them, they know their potential clients don't want to hear from another pushy sales person. Besides, we set up our businesses based on our passion, because we want to help others and change the world, and we don't want to sound like second-hand car salesmen!

Many of my clients find themselves in a catch 22: they know their product or service is excellent but clients only realize and appreciate the value once they've experienced the product. Unable to clearly explain this amazing value to their potential clients, they have to constantly decrease their price just to make a sale.

Smart Business System™

The solution is the **21st Century Sales Formula™**, which is about helping your potential clients in advance so you show them, before asking for the sale, that you are the right person to help them.

The secret is to do it in such a way that you **create interest for your product or service so you don't even have to "sell" for a sale to happen**.

Imagine your best clients coming to you and begging you to sell to them!

Join my next Master Class on How to Accelerate Your Sales **(www.ozanagiusca.com/accelerate-sales)** to discover how easy this is. And yes, this is exactly what I do – I create interest and earn the trust of potential clients (like you) by offering real help in my Master Classes without any sales talk.

The more value you create in your marketplace, the more offers you can make. And of course, the more offers you make, the more sales you can achieve.

21st Century Sales Formula™

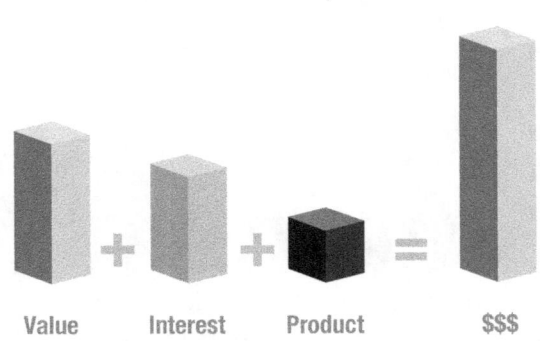

Value   Interest   Product $$$

Challenge #5

Most people in business have invested money, time and a lot of efforts in promotion, but the results are far from satisfying. This is because many tactics have been used in isolation without a strategy to back them up.

If you feel you have this challenge, then I highly encourage you to discover my Ads into Profit Blueprint™, where you can get answers to your burning questions about advertising, and more importantly, where

Business Unlimited

you can ask more questions to help you get the RIGHT answers. Yes, it is only when you ask yourself the right questions that you can get helpful answers, so you can really get a good return on their promo budget.

Access Ads into Profits Master Class *(www.ozanagiusca.com/turn-ads-into-profitable-customers)* to get the right answers to the right questions.

Most entrepreneurs gain business in the traditional way. What you'll understand is how to expand beyond what you do well and break through the current sales figure, by adding other products, services, actions.

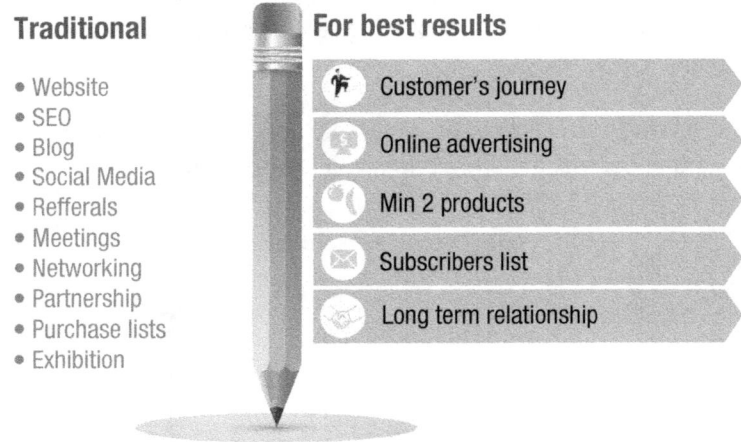

Traditional
- Website
- SEO
- Blog
- Social Media
- Refferals
- Meetings
- Networking
- Partnership
- Purchase lists
- Exhibition

For best results
- Customer's journey
- Online advertising
- Min 2 products
- Subscribers list
- Long term relationship

Challenge #6

Most people in business have a lot to do and not enough time to do it! They wish the working day had 48 hours so they could hold more meetings with potential clients and show their product to more people; to ultimately increase their sales and profits.

Well, there is a way for you to have 50 to 500 sales conversations in an hour or so. If you're asking yourself how this is possible, the **10x Events System™** *(www.ozanagiusca.com/10x-sales-bootcamp-en)* is for you.

Instead of giving away valuable information about your product or service during a sales conversation, share it in an educational or fun context, when your potential clients WANT to hear you talk about your offering.

The benefit of selling at events is that it is the most efficient way to sell, while getting your potential clients to love you for the experience and information you provide.

What do I mean by 'events'? It could be a workshop, a webinar, a series of online videos, a sampling / tasting or networking event, even a fashion show.

As you become closer to being an important player in your niche, you need to consider selling from the stage/ via events. This is not just for experts and trainers. Our clients who have introduced events in their marketing and selling activities include fashion, car repair, consultants, kids development, agricultural equipment, even doctors.

Of course, we are not talking about just any event! There is a way to hold events of the highest quality, which I share with you in the **10x Events System™** *(www.ozanagiusca.com/10x-sales-bootcamp-en)*.

Challenge #7

Whether an established business or a newcomer, we all want to make more money. For some, money is a means to living the desired lifestyle, and for others it's a means to show they've achieved a lot and gained the appreciation and respect they deserve.

The challenges are that due to daily activities, and fires that need to be put out, entrepreneurs forget about their destination and most often behave as if lost in a dark forest.

In addition, in a world with so many people trying to sell so much it is difficult to grab your clients' attention. In a world where it is hard to get the right employees, and where communication is so important... it is not easy to 'construct' the right messages that attract the right people. You need to formulate your messages, with a view to ensuring that they are short and to the point, but most importantly, that they get to the heart of your potential clients. Such communication depends on the clarity you have about yourself and your business, and the connection between the two.

Smart Business System™

Unless you have a set of key messages that you and your team consistently use, you are just another seller, talking in generic terms like most people. This means you are forced to keep your price to a minimum, rather than getting paid for the real value you provide.

In other words, you need to carefully draft your key messages to use as your introduction, as a conversation opener or even on stage when you speak in front of more people. In order to get it right, you need to go to the essence of your business.

This is YOUR job!

No external consultants can come up with your key messages because they have to represent you. And the good news is that when you work on identifying such messages, you'll reconnect with your business and fall in love with it all over again.

The outcome is the right foundation for your communication, and you'll really become unstoppable and truly fulfilled when you answer the 7 WHY-based questions shown in the illustration below.

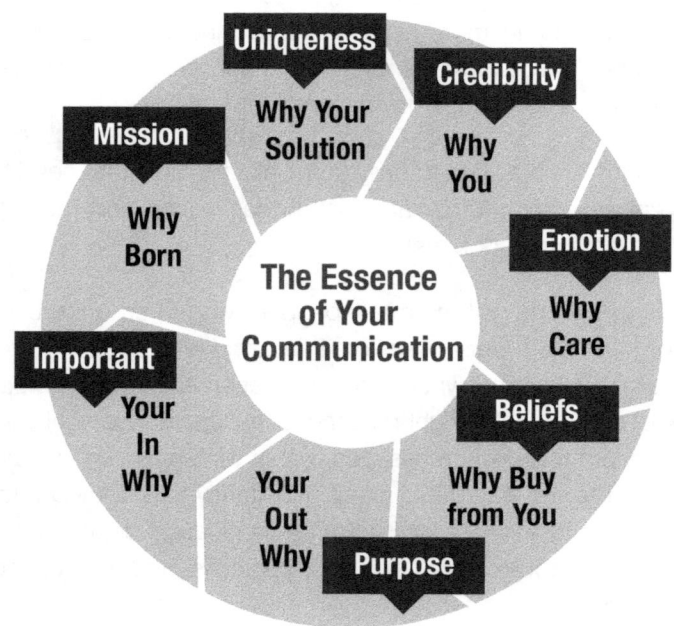

Big companies spent tens of thousands of dollars to identify their key messages. We've created a process to help you distill your key messages without spending an arm and a leg.

Would you like to overcome any of these challenges?

Then I invite you to join my **Smart Business Accelerator™** *(www.ozanagiusca.com/kim-en)* to discover how to build your Smarter Business, your business anchored in the current reality, and adapted to your current needs, aligned to your heart, so you feel in control and get to your destination faster.

Let's spend two days together, and you will

- Evaluate your growth opportunities to unleash the full potential of your business

- Eliminate time wasters, so you really focus on what is most important for you

Leave this workshop with clarity, ways to upgrade your business and a plan of action so you achieve your objectives faster.

Bonus: Love Letter

More value to you

I write about giving more Value than anticipated to your clients, about amazing your customers, about giving something for free. Here, it is my freebie to wow you.

Following, you will find the easieast way to come up with your marketing strategy. I give you the tool so you define your marketing strategy in 30 minutes. The tool is in the form of a letter you write to yourself as if it was written by your Best Customer. I call it 'Love Letter' because it shows the love your customers have to your company. It looks like a testimonial, but it is much more than that. Fill in the blanks. The point of this letter is to help you really understand your business, and what matters for your business's success. It looks like a testimonial, but it is way more than that. Once this letter sounds right, you know the recipe for your business's success. You have more clarity about your own business. You just need to execute correctly (You can do that by applying the 101 tactics in this book).

Below you will find a template for your Love Letter, as well as the letter I wrote for Tooliers®. This helps me 'name' my Persona, the benefits of my product (both logical and emotional), the impact my product has on customers' lives, how to find our customers, what to use to find customers, what I want my customers journey to be, how to ask them to provide recommendations, and more.

This template is your Strategy in a nutshell! And yes, you can use this to get inspiration for what you want your (real) client testimonials to look like.

I challenge you to fill in the blanks for your business. If you want the original, so you don't have to type up the template, visit **www.ozanagiusca.com/love-letter/** and grab your copy for free.

Love Letter Template

Dear **[Company Name]**,

My name is **[Persona's name]** and I must tell you I love your **[product type]** and I feel compelled to tell you my story.

I am a **[business type / life or lifestyle role]** who **[problem / passion statement]**. Thing is, that **[impact of pain / passion to life]**.

But **[Product Name]** changed my life.

Whenever I **[do specific things with product]** it works exactly as promised. Not only do I **[specific benefits]** but it makes me feel **[strong emotional reaction]**.

I find I use the product in that way every **[time period: hour / day / week, etc.]**

It's as if you looked me in the eye and said, '**[Persona's name]**, I promise you **[value promise]**'.

What I didn't expect, and share with other **[why shares with]** by **[mean of 'sharing']** is that you made me feel **[emotion impact]**.

Your product has forever **[how life changed]**.

I first heard of your product while **[activity / place related to title or life role]**. I decided to learn if it was really meant for me, so **[how to get more info]** where you said **[key message promise],** which spoke directly to me. To tell you the truth, at first I was skeptical. But then, when you provided **[activity to induce trust]** I knew you were the right company.

[Influencer] endorsing the product was also key.

Still, I felt **[primary concern / objection]**.

Finally, when **[final action]** I was ready to **[sign up / buy / try]**.

I couldn't wait to get going, so as soon as I could, I **[first product setup / interaction]** to get started, and very quickly tried the **[feature to realize promise]** which made me feel hopeful that I had made the right decision.

Love Letter Example

Dear Tooliers®,

My name is Elisabeth. I must tell you that I love your Marketing Lens™ Diagnosis and Growth Program and I feel compelled to tell you my story.

I am an accounting firm owner who needs more clients. Thing is, I'm not earning enough. But Marketing Lens™ has changed my life.

Whenever I think of investing in marketing activities, I use the Marketing Lens™ and it works exactly as promised. Not only do I discover free ways to attract clients, but it also makes me feel like I really master marketing as a whole. I find myself working on one action to grow my business every other day, for only 15 minutes per day. I started this just one month ago and I already see 10% more enquiries from potential clients.

It's as if you looked me in the eye and said, 'Elisabeth I promise that you will discover ways of getting more customers by yourself without spending a cent.'

What I didn't expect, and I share this with other accounting firm owners in our regular ACCA meetings, is that you made me feel like a great businessperson, not just an accountant. I truly *feel* I own my business now; I am not just a simple accountant who has a job in my own company.

Marketing Lens™ Diagnosis and Growth Program has forever changed how I market our accounting services.

I first heard of your product while browsing The American Institute of CPAs online. I decided to learn if it was really meant for me and I went to www.tooliers.com. You said that I would get answers to questions I had never asked myself and this really resonated with me. To tell you the truth, at first I was skeptical about getting actions tailored to my business and given automatically to me by a computer! No one knows my industry better than me. But then, when you provided the Marketing Lens™ Diagnostic Report I knew you were the right company. Your assessment of why I was not attracting the customers I wanted was spot on. You also showed me what I need to focus on attracting the customers I deserve.

Entrepreneur.com's endorsement of Marketing Lens™ Diagnosis and Growth Program was also key to my decision to check you out. They are a trusted resource with information for every business owner.

Still, even at this stage I felt marketing was too complicated for me. Besides, I truly love performing accounting services, *not* marketing my business. Finally, after having followed the Action Plan on Social Media, I was ready to buy the Marketing Lens™ Growth Program. I understand now that things are not as complicated as they seemed, and that even I can attract and engage online with potential clients for my firm!

I couldn't wait to get going, so as soon as I could, I performed the Marketing Lens™ Diagnosis. I quickly started with the first action on Sales Funnel Tactic, which made me feel comfortable that I'd made the right decision. I see how, by the end of the Growth Program, I will have become a marketing guru for my business; customers will come to us, as bees are attracted to a honeypot. And you know what? I now see myself as *managing an accounting practice*, and no longer as doing accounting services. The latter is the job of my employees!

Love Letter

> **Want to grow your business and don't know how and where to start?**

> **Or do you have a business challenge you want an expert opinion on?**

I love bringing new ideas to the table and contributing to the growth of any kind of business, from e-commerce sites to professional services providers; from retail to entertainment. Every industry has its own particularities, but all have one thing in common: **apply best business practices and your business will succeed.** It's exactly this subject that I've mastered, and I can help any business implement best practices, regardless of size, industry or geography.

So contact me via my website and I'll respond within 24 hours.

www.ozanagiusca.com

If you just want to stay in touch, connect with me on:

- www.facebook.com/giusca.ozana
- plus.google.com/+OzanaGiusca
- www.linkedin.com/in/ozanagiusca
- www.twitter.com/OzanaGiusca
- www.youtube.com/user/ozana197

Glossary of Terms

These definitions are crafted to be as simple as possible, and are explained in the context of this book.

AAA rating - refers to the evaluation of credit worthiness; i.e how trustworthy a company is to do business with. The highest rating is AAA, descending to C (low) and D (even worse).

Action Plan or Fast Track implementation Plan - a step-by-step guide to work on and improve various areas of the business (strategy, sales, marketing, etc.) and sub-areas (educational marketing, writing blogs, building a website, email marketing etc.).

Affiliate Marketing - this is an agreement whereby a business rewards someone (affiliate person or company) for each visitor / customer brought by the affiliate's own marketing efforts, or for each purchase generated by the affiliate, within a time frame.

Attractive Premium - an item included in a pack, together with less interesting items, and sold as a bundle. It's a good way of moving slow-selling products.

Automate / Automating / Automation - using software rather than employees to undertake automatically some processes within the company.

Business-to-business (B2B) - a business that sells to other businesses. Compare with Business-to-Consumer (B2C), which is when the company sells to consumers / individuals.

Better Offer - a product (service) or a bundle of products (services), designed to offer more value (than usual) for the same dollar spent.

Brand - the name, design, symbol, colors or any other feature that identifies one company or product. For example, Coca-Cola is one brand, Fanta is another; they both belong to The Coca-Cola Company.

Branding via Association - linking the brand of one business with a better known brand, so the lesser known brand 'borrows' from the popularity of the other.

Business Doctor - business growth solution consisting of (i) diagnosing a business (see Business Lens®), (ii) designing a customized action plan to optimize and grow the company and (iii) implementing that plan.

Business Lens® - company assessment toolkit to show business owners the naked truth about their company. It identifies unexploited growth potential. It covers everything that matters for the growth of the business (analyzes in detail 15 business dimensions, including Strategy, Innovation, Leadership, Superstar Organization, Marketing, Sales, Human Resources, Motivation, Support Systems, Follow-Up and Organizational Culture) a Tooliers® service.

Business Lens® Diagnostic - the process of answering multiple choice questions and getting a business evaluation report that shows what the business does well and what it needs to focus on a Tooliers® service.

Buying Criteria - the requirements and rules that one buyer uses to buy a product, such as quality, price, availability, reliability, durability, comfort, habit, safety, freshness, coolness, taste, production methods, etc.

Chunking - grouping together information into ideally sized pieces, so they can be used effectively to produce the outcome one wants without stress or shutdown.

Chunk Down - dealing with smaller parts of information / activities in order to understand or do them effectively. Especially useful when the information / activities are new or complex.

Chunk Up - dealing with larger parts of information / activities in order to understand / accomplish more at once. Especially useful when one faces known information or deals with routine activities

Complementary Product (Service) - product (service) whose use is interrelated with the use of another product (service); e.g. cartridges and printers are complementary products.

Cross Selling - one business selling its product (service) to another business's customers, and vice versa.

Distribution Channel - the path through which products travel from vendors to consumers; e.g. coffee travels from farmer to exporter, to importer, to distributor, and to the retailer who sells to the end user.

Educational Marketing - sharing valuable information with potential customers, for their benefit and to build trust.

Gift with Purchase - providing another product (service) when someone buys a certain product (service); e.g. a sample cream when you buy a perfume.

Host-Parasite Relationship - adding one's product to be sold passively together with another product that is marketed and sold by the other business (the 'parasite' company doesn't do anything to make sales happen). E.g. producer of a dress adds belt from another manufacturer,

and promotes and sells the dress with the belt.

Inducement(s) - an incentive to make the offering more appealing to the customer, and the sale sweeter.

Joined Offers - offering one's product together with another product; both parties promote the combined offer.

Joint Venture (JV) - business agreement for a set period, in which each party undertakes some efforts, for the benefit of all parties.

Lead - term used for a potential customer in the first stage of a sales process; i.e. the business made the initial contact with that prospect, be it (directly or indirectly) via the business's website, or via a phone call or meeting.

Lead Nurturing Email - email designed to build relationships and trust with prospective customers in a consistent and relevant manner.

Limited Edition - the manufacturing of a product in a limited quantity, to make it a more interesting purchase for the buyer.

Limited Time Offer - an offer that has a specific deadline, to give potential buyers a clear reason to act without delay.

Limited Stock Offer - a limited number of items made available, to give potential buyers a clear reason to act without delay.

Locking Sales In - securing long-term sales; e.g. signing a long-term contract or ensuring customer comes back for repeat purchase.

Offer Email - an email to promote a product, to ask for a purchase.

Potentials or Prospects - potential customers.

Pre-emptive Anti-competition Strategy - a strategy employed by one business to lead potentials to only consider its offering, thus blocking its competitors even before they are considered by the buyer as potential sellers.

Risk Reversal - marketing strategy based on removing the risks of the buyer to help them make the purchase decision; e.g. 30-day money back guarantee.

ROI (Return on Investment) - a performance measure calculated as the benefit produced by an investment divided by the cost of that investment (expressed as %); commonly used to evaluate the efficiency of an investment or to compare different real or potential investments.

Glossary of Terms

ROTI (Return on Time Invested) - the return on the time invested into an activity or project (valued in dollar amount per hour).

Sales Funnel - a metaphoric description of the sales process from initial contact to final sale. It is called a 'funnel', because there are many leads (cold potentials), and as one gets closer to the sale, the number decreases.

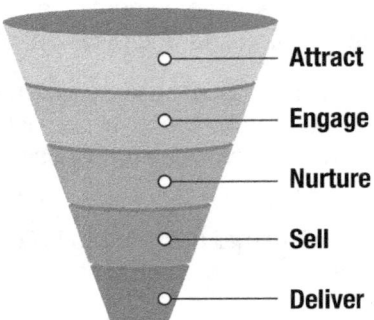

Soft Skills - a cluster of personality traits, social abilities, communication, language, and personal habits that characterize relationships of one person with others.

Tooliers® - online platform with business growth tools designed to help small and mid-sized business owners to take their companies to the next level. Founded by Ozana Gusca.

Ultimate Strategic Position (USP) (not to be confused with Unique Selling Proposition) – the final perception that a company wants to have in the eyes of the customer.

Unique Value Proposition (UVP) - a few words used by one business to tell prospective customers why they should buy their product or use their service; it tells how this business adds more value or better solves a problem than competing businesses (similar to Unique Selling Proposition).

Value Papers - promotional materials (such as flyers, leaflets, brochures, catalogues) that give, besides the usual information / advertising content, monetary value to the holder towards the purchase of the product / service being promoted (such as % discount, $ reduction, gift); the goal is to incentivize a sale.

'Any ending is a new beginning.'
Ozana Giusca

Make the most of the knowledge you have received or gotten from this book and take your business to the next level.

In this series

www.ozanagiusca.com/BusinessUnlimited

www.ingramcontent.com/pod-product-compliance
Lightning Source LLC
Chambersburg PA
CBHW070306230526
45470CB00002B/746